The Ultimate Guide to TikTok Growth: Tips and Ideas for Building Your Following

Welcome to "The Ultimate Guide to TikTok Growth: Tips and Ideas for Building Your Following." TikTok has become one of the fastest-growing social media platforms in the world, with millions of users worldwide. Whether you're an influencer, a business owner, or just looking to build your personal brand, TikTok is an excellent tool for reaching a large and engaged audience.

But with so many users on the platform, it can be tough to stand out from the crowd and grow your following. That's why we've created this ultimate guide to TikTok growth. In this book, we'll share some tips and ideas for creating content that resonates with your target audience, optimizing your profile for maximum visibility, and using TikTok's unique features to your advantage.

Whether you're just starting out on TikTok or looking to take your presence on the platform to the next level, this guide will provide you with the tools and knowledge you need to succeed. So, let's dive in!

Chapter 1: Introduction to TikTok

TikTok is a social media platform that has taken the world by storm, with over 1 billion active users worldwide. Originally launched in China in 2016 as Douyin, TikTok is a short-form video-sharing app that allows users to create and share 15-60 second videos with music, filters, and other creative tools.

TikTok has become a hub for creativity and entertainment, with a vast range of content from dance videos to comedy sketches, and even educational and informative content. It has become a powerful tool for individuals, businesses, and influencers to reach new audiences and build their brands.

If you are looking to build your following on TikTok, this guide is for you. In the following chapters, we will explore various tips and strategies that you can use to grow your presence on TikTok and reach your target audience.

The rise of TikTok

TikTok is a social media platform that has gained immense popularity in recent years. It was launched in 2016 by the Chinese tech company ByteDance and quickly became a hit in Asia. It wasn't long before it spread across the world, and today, it boasts over a billion active users.

TikTok allows users to create and share short videos with their followers. These videos can be up to 60 seconds long and can include music, filters, special effects, and other features. The app's algorithm is designed to promote engaging content, making it a great platform for creators who want to showcase their skills and creativity.

TikTok's success can be attributed to several factors, including its ease of use, addictive nature, and the way it encourages users to engage with each other. The platform's ability to reach a broad and diverse audience has also made it a powerful marketing tool for businesses and influencers alike.

In this guide, we'll explore some of the most effective strategies for growing your TikTok following and building a successful presence on the platform. Whether you're a business owner, a content creator, or just someone who wants to have fun on TikTok, this guide has everything you need to know to get started.

Demographics of TikTok users

TikTok has a wide range of users across different age groups, genders, and geographic locations. According to recent data, the majority of TikTok users are between the ages of 16 and 24. However, the app's popularity is also growing among older age groups. In terms of gender, TikTok has a fairly balanced user base, with roughly an equal number of male and female users.

TikTok's popularity is also global, with users from all over the world. The app has particularly gained traction in Asia, with a large user base in China, where the app originated as Douyin. However, it has also become increasingly popular in other regions such as North America, Europe, and Latin America. This diversity in user demographics presents a unique opportunity for content creators to reach a global audience through the platform.

The potential for businesses and creators on TikTok

TikTok has become a powerful platform for businesses and creators to reach a young and engaged audience. With its rapidly growing user base and powerful algorithm, TikTok has become a force to be reckoned with in the world of social media marketing.

For businesses, TikTok provides a unique opportunity to connect with a younger demographic and build brand awareness in a way that is both fun and engaging. The platform's short-form videos and user-generated content create a sense of authenticity and relatability that is often difficult to achieve through traditional advertising.

For creators, TikTok offers the potential to grow a following quickly and to reach millions of people around the world. The platform's algorithm favors content that is engaging and shareable, making it easier for creators to go viral and build a following.

Whether you are a business or a creator, TikTok provides a powerful platform for building your brand, reaching new audiences, and growing your following. With the right strategy and approach, TikTok can be a game-changer for your social media marketing efforts.

Chapter 2: Understanding TikTok Algorithm

TikTok has become one of the most popular social media platforms, with over 1 billion active users. As a result, it has become a great platform for businesses and creators to grow their following and increase their reach. To achieve this, it is essential to understand how the TikTok algorithm works.

The TikTok algorithm is the system that determines what content appears on a user's "For You" page. The "For You" page is the main feed on TikTok, where users can discover new content that is tailored to their interests. The algorithm uses a combination of factors to determine what content appears on the "For You" page.

Understanding the TikTok algorithm is essential for businesses and creators who want to grow their following and increase their reach. By creating engaging and relevant content that resonates with their audience, businesses and creators can increase their chances of appearing on the "For You" page and reaching new audiences.

How the TikTok algorithm works

The TikTok algorithm is responsible for showing users the videos they are most likely to enjoy based on their interests, viewing history, and engagement with content. The algorithm uses a combination of factors to determine which videos to show to each user.

Some of the key factors that the TikTok algorithm takes into account include:

User interactions: The algorithm looks at the videos that a user has liked, shared, and commented on, and uses this information to suggest similar videos.

Video information: The algorithm analyzes the details of each video, such as captions, hashtags, and sounds, to understand its context and relevance.

Device and account settings: The algorithm considers a user's device type, language preference, and location to provide personalized recommendations.

Popular content: The algorithm takes into account the videos that are currently popular on the platform and may recommend them to users who have shown an interest in similar content.

Completeness of the video: The algorithm prefers videos that are complete and have a clear beginning, middle, and end. Videos that are too short or too long may be deprioritized in the algorithm.

Video quality: The algorithm also takes into account the quality of the video, including its resolution, lighting, and sound quality.

By understanding how the TikTok algorithm works, creators and businesses can optimize their content to reach a wider audience and build a following on the platform.

Factors affecting the TikTok algorithm

There are several factors that can affect the TikTok algorithm and determine how often and to whom your content is shown. Some of these factors include:

User interactions: The algorithm tracks how users engage with your content, such as liking, commenting, sharing, and following your account. The more engagement you receive, the higher your chances of getting your content shown to a wider audience.

Video information: TikTok also analyzes video information, such as captions, sounds, hashtags, and video content. Using relevant hashtags and sounds can help your videos get discovered by users interested in similar content.

Device and account settings: TikTok takes into account the device and account settings of users, such as language preference, country, and device type. This information can impact the types of content shown to users.

Completion rate: The algorithm also tracks how often users watch your entire video. Higher completion rates indicate that users are interested in your content and are more likely to see your future content.

Timeliness: TikTok prioritizes recent content and creators who regularly post new content. Consistently posting high-quality content can help boost your chances of being featured on the "For You" page.

Trending topics: TikTok algorithms also analyze trending topics and popular hashtags, so using them can help increase visibility.

It's important to note that the TikTok algorithm is constantly changing and evolving, so staying up to date on the latest updates and changes is crucial for building and maintaining a following on the platform.

Tips for optimizing content for the algorithm

Here are some tips for optimizing your TikTok content for the algorithm:

Use popular songs and sounds: TikTok's algorithm favors content that uses popular songs and sounds, so try to incorporate them into your videos.

Keep your videos short: TikTok's algorithm tends to favor shorter videos, so aim for videos that are around 15-60 seconds in length.

Use eye-catching thumbnails: Your video's thumbnail is the first thing people see, so make sure it's eye-catching and accurately represents your video's content.

Use relevant hashtags: Use relevant hashtags that are related to your video's content. This will help your videos appear in relevant search results and increase their visibility.

Post at peak times: TikTok's algorithm favors accounts that post frequently and consistently, so try to post during peak times when your audience is most active.

Engage with your audience: Engage with your audience by responding to comments and messages. This will help build a loyal following and increase the likelihood of your content being shared.

Use TikTok trends: Keep an eye on current TikTok trends and challenges, and try to incorporate them into your videos. This will increase the likelihood of your content being seen by a wider audience.

By following these tips, you can increase the visibility of your TikTok content and optimize it for the algorithm.

VIKASH DABRIWAL

Chapter 3: Creating Engaging Content

TikTok is all about creating short, engaging videos that capture people's attention and keep them entertained. With millions of users and countless videos posted every day, it's essential to create content that stands out and engages your audience. In this chapter, we'll explore some tips and ideas for creating engaging content on TikTok.

Know your audience

One of the most important things to consider when creating content for TikTok is your target audience. Who are you trying to reach, and what kind of content do they enjoy? Take some time to research the interests and preferences of your audience and tailor your content accordingly.

Use trending sounds and hashtags

TikTok is all about trends, and using popular sounds and hashtags can help your content get noticed by a wider audience. Keep an eye on the latest trends and incorporate them into your videos whenever possible.

Be creative and original

While it's important to follow trends and use popular sounds and hashtags, it's also essential to be creative and original. Don't be afraid to try new things and experiment with different types of content. TikTok is a platform that values creativity, so the more unique and original your content is, the better.

Keep it short and sweet

One of the most appealing aspects of TikTok is its short-form video format. Most TikTok videos are under 60 seconds long, and many are much shorter. Keep this in mind when creating your content and try to keep your videos concise and to the point.

Use eye-catching visuals

TikTok is a visual platform, so it's important to use eye-catching visuals in your videos. This could include interesting camera angles, creative editing, or unique filters and effects.

Tell a story

While TikTok videos are short, they can still tell a story. Consider using your videos to tell a narrative or convey a message. This can help your content resonate with viewers and make them more likely to engage with your content.

Be authentic

Finally, it's important to be authentic when creating content on TikTok. Users can quickly tell when content is fake or forced, so be genuine and let your personality shine through in your videos. This can help you build a loyal following of fans who appreciate your unique voice and perspective.

By following these tips and ideas, you can create engaging and entertaining content that will help you build a following on TikTok. In the next chapter, we'll explore some strategies for promoting your content and growing your audience on the platform.

Types of content that perform well on TikTok

There are several types of content that tend to perform well on TikTok:

Challenges: Challenges are popular on TikTok and can help your content reach a wider audience. You can create your own challenge or participate in a popular one.

Dances: Dancing is a big part of TikTok culture and can be a great way to showcase your personality and creativity.

Educational content: Educational content is popular on TikTok, particularly if it's presented in a fun and engaging way.

Comedy: TikTok is known for its humorous content, so if you have a knack for making people laugh, this could be a great avenue for you.

Lip syncing: Lip syncing is a popular TikTok trend, particularly with popular songs and dialogue from movies and TV shows.

Duets: Duets allow you to collaborate with another TikTok user, which can help to expand your audience and increase engagement.

Behind-the-scenes: Giving your audience a glimpse into your life or creative process can help to build a connection with them and keep them engaged.

Short skits: Creating short skits or scenes can be a great way to showcase your creativity and storytelling skills.

DIY and tutorials: DIY and tutorial videos are popular on TikTok and can help to showcase your skills and knowledge in a particular area.

Product demonstrations: If you're promoting a product or service, creating a demonstration video can be a great way to showcase its benefits and features.

Best practices for creating engaging content

Here are some best practices for creating engaging content on TikTok:

Keep it short and sweet: TikTok videos are typically short, so it's important to get your message across quickly and efficiently. Aim for videos that are between 15 and 60 seconds long.

Use eye-catching visuals: TikTok is a highly visual platform, so use eye-catching visuals and bright colors to grab the attention of viewers. You can use filters, effects, and text overlays to make your content stand out.

Be authentic and relatable: TikTok users love authenticity and relatability, so be yourself and showcase your personality. Share real-life moments, behind-the-scenes footage, or your daily routine.

Tell a story: People love stories, so try to tell a story with your content. It could be a story about your life, your brand, or your product. Make it interesting and engaging to keep viewers hooked.

Use humor: TikTok is a platform that loves humor, so don't be afraid to inject some humor into your content. Make people laugh and they'll be more likely to share your content.

Incorporate music: Music is a big part of the TikTok experience, so use music that fits your content and matches the mood you're trying to create. You can use popular songs, trending sounds, or create your own original music.

Use calls-to-action: Encourage engagement with your content by using calls-to-action. Ask viewers to like, comment, or share your content, or direct them to your website or other social media channels.

Experiment with different formats: TikTok offers a variety of formats, including duets, reactions, challenges, and more. Experiment with different formats to see what works best for your brand or content.

Tips for finding your niche on TikTok

Finding your niche on TikTok is essential for building a loyal following and standing out from the millions of other users on the platform. Here are some tips for finding your niche:

Explore different content categories: Take the time to explore the different types of content on TikTok, such as dancing, comedy, beauty, food, and DIY. See what content resonates with you and what you enjoy creating.

Identify your skills and passions: Consider your skills, hobbies, and interests, and think about how you can translate them into compelling content on TikTok. If you love to cook, for example, you might create recipe videos or share cooking tips and tricks.

Look at what's trending: Keep an eye on the latest TikTok trends and challenges, and see if there's a way to put your own unique spin on them. You can also create content around popular hashtags to increase your visibility.

Analyze your audience: Pay attention to who is engaging with your content and what they are responding to. Use this information to tailor your content to their interests and preferences.

Be authentic: Don't try to force a particular niche if it doesn't feel authentic to you. Be true to yourself and your interests, and your audience will appreciate the genuine content you create.

Remember that finding your niche is an ongoing process, and it's okay to experiment with different types of content until you find what works best for you.

Chapter 4: Building Your Brand on TikTok

Great! Here's Chapter 4 on "Building Your Brand on TikTok":

TikTok has become a popular platform for businesses and creators to build their brand and grow their audience. With the app's immense reach and virality, it offers a unique opportunity to connect with a large and engaged audience.

Here are some tips for building your brand on TikTok:

Define Your Brand

Before you start creating content, it's important to have a clear understanding of your brand and what you stand for. This will help you create content that is consistent with your brand and resonates with your audience.

Some questions to ask yourself when defining your brand include:

What is the purpose of my brand?

What are my core values?

Who is my target audience?

What makes my brand unique?

Create a Content Strategy

Once you have a clear understanding of your brand, it's time to create a content strategy. This involves identifying the types of content you want to create, the frequency of your posts, and the tone and style of your content.

When creating your content strategy, it's important to consider your audience's interests and preferences. Look at what is currently trending on TikTok and find ways to incorporate these trends into your content.

Consistency is Key

Consistency is key when it comes to building your brand on TikTok. Post regularly and at consistent intervals to keep your audience engaged and build a following.

It's also important to maintain a consistent tone and style in your content. This will help your audience recognize your brand and build a sense of familiarity and trust.

Engage with Your Audience

Engagement is a crucial aspect of building your brand on TikTok. Respond to comments, like and share other users' content, and participate in challenges and trends.

When you engage with your audience, you build a sense of community and connection. This can help increase your reach and build a loyal following.

Collaborate with Other Creators

Collaborating with other creators is a great way to build your brand on TikTok. By collaborating with other creators in your niche, you can tap into their audience and reach new followers.

When collaborating with other creators, make sure their content is aligned with your brand and values. This will help ensure that your collaboration is successful and well-received by your audience.

In conclusion, building your brand on TikTok takes time and effort, but it can be an incredibly rewarding experience. By defining your brand, creating a content strategy, being consistent, engaging with your audience, and collaborating with other creators, you can build a strong and loyal following on the app.

Strategies for building a strong brand on TikTok

Building a strong brand on TikTok involves more than just creating engaging content. It requires a well-thought-out strategy and a clear understanding of your target audience. Here are some strategies for building your brand on TikTok:

Define your brand: Start by defining what your brand is all about. What are your values, mission, and vision? What sets you apart from other brands? This will help you create content that is aligned with your brand and resonates with your audience.

Develop a content strategy: Develop a content strategy that is aligned with your brand and target audience. Determine what type of content you want to create and how often you will post. Be sure to include a mix of content, including educational, entertaining, and promotional content.

Use hashtags: Use relevant hashtags to make it easier for your target audience to find your content. Research popular hashtags in your niche and include them in your posts.

Collaborate with other creators: Collaborating with other creators can help you reach a wider audience and build relationships with other creators. Look for creators who have a similar audience to yours and reach out to them to collaborate on a video.

Engage with your audience: Engage with your audience by responding to comments and messages. This will help you build relationships with your followers and create a sense of community around your brand.

Analyze your metrics: Use TikTok's analytics to track your metrics and see what's working and what's not. This will help you adjust your content strategy and make data-driven decisions.

Stay authentic: Finally, stay authentic to your brand and your audience. Don't try to be someone you're not or create content that doesn't align with your brand values. Authenticity is key to building a strong brand on TikTok.

Tips for creating a consistent brand image

Here are some tips for creating a consistent brand image on TikTok:

Develop a unique visual style: Use consistent colors, fonts, and design elements in your videos to make them instantly recognizable as part of your brand.

Use branded hashtags: Create a hashtag that represents your brand and use it consistently in all of your videos. Encourage your followers to use the hashtag when they share content related to your brand.

Collaborate with other brands and creators: Collaborating with other brands and creators on TikTok can help you reach new audiences and build your brand image. Look for other brands and creators whose values align with your own.

Be authentic: TikTok users value authenticity and genuine interactions. Avoid coming across as overly promotional or inauthentic in your videos.

Engage with your followers: Respond to comments and messages from your followers, and ask for their feedback on your content. Engaging with your audience can help you build a loyal fan base and improve your content over time.

Consistently post high-quality content: Posting high-quality content on a consistent basis can help you build your brand and attract new followers. Make sure your content is visually appealing, well-edited, and adds value to your audience.

By implementing these strategies, you can create a strong and consistent brand image on TikTok that resonates with your target audience.

Utilizing TikTok trends and challenges to enhance your brand

One effective way to boost your brand on TikTok is to participate in popular trends and challenges. This can help increase your visibility and engagement, as well as show that your brand is up-to-date and relevant.

Here are some tips for utilizing TikTok trends and challenges to enhance your brand:

Stay up-to-date with the latest trends: Keep an eye on what's popular on TikTok by regularly browsing the "For You" page and following relevant accounts in your industry. This can help you identify trends and challenges that align with your brand and messaging.

Put your own spin on it: While it's important to follow the rules of the trend or challenge, don't be afraid to put your own unique twist on it. This can help you stand out from the crowd and make your content more memorable.

Use relevant hashtags: Hashtags can help increase the reach of your content and make it easier for users to find you. Make sure to use relevant hashtags when participating in trends and challenges, as well as in your regular content.

Stay true to your brand: While it's important to participate in trends and challenges, make sure to stay true to your brand's voice and messaging. This can help you build a loyal following and avoid appearing inauthentic.

Collaborate with others: Consider collaborating with other creators or brands when participating in trends and challenges. This can help you reach a wider audience and build new relationships in your industry.

Chapter 5: Collaborating with Other TikTok Creators

Collaborating with other TikTok creators can be a great way to expand your reach and gain new followers. By partnering with other creators who share your niche or audience, you can create content that is both engaging and mutually beneficial.

Here are some tips for successful collaboration on TikTok:

Find the right partner: Look for creators who share your values and niche, and whose audience aligns with yours. You can reach out to them directly or through TikTok's duet or collaboration features.

Plan your content: Collaborate on a specific theme or challenge, and plan your content together. This will ensure that your content is cohesive and aligned with your brand and niche.

Cross-promote: When you post your collaboration video, be sure to tag your partner and encourage your followers to check out their content. This will help to grow both of your audiences.

Be creative: Think outside the box and come up with unique ideas for collaboration. This will make your content stand out and keep your audience engaged.

Communicate effectively: Keep the lines of communication open throughout the collaboration process. Make sure you both have a clear understanding of the content you will be creating and the timeline for posting.

By collaborating with other TikTok creators, you can leverage their audience to grow your own and create content that is fresh and exciting. Just remember to choose your partners wisely, plan your content carefully, and communicate effectively throughout the process.

The benefits of collaborating with other TikTok creators

Collaborating with other TikTok creators can offer many benefits, including:

Increased exposure: By collaborating with other creators, you can tap into their audience and potentially gain new followers for your own account. This can help you reach a wider audience and increase your visibility on the platform.

Creativity: Collaborating with others can inspire you to create new and innovative content that you may not have thought of on your own. It can also provide an opportunity to explore new styles or genres that you may not have tried before.

Networking: Collaborating with other creators can help you build relationships within the TikTok community. This can lead to new opportunities, such as future collaborations, sponsorships, or other partnerships.

Learning from others: Collaborating with other creators can provide an opportunity to learn new skills or techniques from other TikTok users. This can help you improve your own content and expand your knowledge of the platform.

Fun: Collaborating with other creators can be a fun and enjoyable experience. It can provide an opportunity to work with like-minded individuals who share a passion for creating content on TikTok.

Overall, collaborating with other TikTok creators can be a great way to enhance your brand, build your audience, and expand your creativity on the platform.

Tips for finding and approaching potential collaborators

Here are some tips for finding and approaching potential collaborators on TikTok:

Use relevant hashtags: Look for popular hashtags related to your niche or industry and search through the videos under those hashtags. This can help you find creators who are making similar content to yours.

Reach out to creators directly: Once you have identified some potential collaborators, reach out to them through direct message. Be sure to personalize your message and explain why you want to collaborate with them. You can also offer some ideas for collaboration to make it easier for them to say yes.

Join collaboration groups: Many TikTok creators form groups specifically for collaboration purposes. You can search for these groups on social media platforms or join TikTok-specific groups. This is a great way to find like-minded creators who are open to collaborating.

Attend TikTok meetups and events: TikTok events are great opportunities to meet other creators and network. Attend these events if possible and make sure to bring your business cards or contact information to exchange with other creators.

Be open to collaboration ideas: When you find a potential collaborator, be open to their ideas for collaboration. This can help to create a more dynamic and unique partnership.

Best practices for successful collaborations

When it comes to successful collaborations on TikTok, there are several best practices to keep in mind:

Clearly define goals and expectations: Before starting a collaboration, make sure you and your partner(s) have a clear understanding of what you hope to achieve and what each person's role will be.

Choose partners with complementary styles and audiences: Look for collaborators who have a similar style or aesthetic to yours, but who also have a different audience that you can reach.

Communicate regularly: Keep in touch with your collaborators throughout the process to ensure everyone is on the same page and any issues are addressed quickly.

Be open to feedback and compromise: Collaboration is about finding common ground and working together, so be willing to listen to others' ideas and make compromises if necessary.

Promote each other's content: Share your partner's content on your own channel and encourage your followers to check out their content. This can help both of you gain new followers and increase engagement.

Have fun: Collaboration should be an enjoyable and creative process, so don't forget to have fun and enjoy the experience!

Chapter 6: Leveraging TikTok Analytics

TikTok provides users with a range of analytics tools to help track their performance and better understand their audience. These insights are crucial for optimizing your content, identifying areas for improvement, and growing your following. In this chapter, we'll explore how to effectively leverage TikTok analytics to achieve your goals.

Understanding TikTok Analytics TikTok Analytics provides a range of insights into your content and audience, including:

Profile overview: This section provides an overview of your profile's performance, including your total number of followers, profile views, and video views.

Content insights: This section provides detailed information about your videos, including views, likes, comments, shares, and engagement rates.

Follower insights: This section provides information about your followers, including their location, gender, and interests.

Trending videos: This section highlights the top-performing videos on TikTok.

Using Analytics to Optimize Your Content Once you understand how to read TikTok Analytics, you can use this data to optimize your content and improve your performance. Some tips for using analytics to optimize your content include:

Identify your top-performing videos: Look at your top-performing videos and try to identify what made them successful. Were they funny, informative, or visually appealing? Once you understand what works, you can create more content in a similar vein.

Track engagement rates: Engagement rate is a key metric for measuring the success of your content. Use analytics to track engagement rates across all of your videos and identify trends. This will help you understand what types of content are resonating with your audience.

Experiment with different content types: Use analytics to experiment with different types of content, such as tutorials, behind-the-scenes footage, or product demos. Pay attention to how your audience responds to each type of content, and use this data to inform your content strategy.

Optimize posting times: Use analytics to identify when your audience is most active on TikTok. This will help you determine the best times to post new content to maximize engagement.

Using Analytics to Understand Your Audience TikTok Analytics also provides valuable insights into your audience. You can use this information to better understand your followers, create content that resonates with them, and attract new followers. Some tips for using analytics to understand your audience include:

Identify your audience demographics: Use analytics to identify the age, gender, location, and interests of your audience. This information can help you tailor your content to better appeal to your target demographic.

Pay attention to trending topics: Use analytics to identify trending topics and themes that your audience is interested in. This will help you create content that is more likely to resonate with your followers.

Monitor follower growth: Use analytics to track your follower growth over time. This will help you identify which types of content and strategies are most effective for growing your audience.

Using Analytics to Track Your Progress Finally, TikTok Analytics is a valuable tool for tracking your progress over time. You can use this data to set goals, measure your progress, and identify areas for improvement. Some tips for using analytics to track your progress include:

Set goals: Use analytics to set specific, measurable goals for your TikTok performance. This could include increasing your follower count, improving your engagement rate, or creating a certain number of videos per week.

Monitor your progress: Regularly review your analytics data to track your progress toward your goals. Use this information to make adjustments to your content strategy and ensure you're on track to meet your objectives.

Identify areas for improvement: Use analytics to identify areas where you need to improve. This could include creating more engaging content, posting more frequently, or experimenting with new content types.

Understanding TikTok analytics and metrics

TikTok provides various metrics and analytics to help users understand how their content is performing on the platform. Here are some of the key metrics and analytics you should know:

Views: The total number of times your videos have been viewed.

Followers: The total number of users following your TikTok account.

Engagement rate: The percentage of your audience that engages with your content, typically measured by likes, comments, shares, and saves.

Impressions: The number of times your content has been displayed to users.

Top territories: The countries or regions where your content is most popular.

Video completion rate: The percentage of viewers who watched your video in full.

Follower growth: The rate at which your follower count is increasing or decreasing.

Audience demographics: Insights into the age, gender, and location of your audience.

Hashtag analytics: The number of times your branded hashtag has been used and the total views generated by the hashtag.

By analyzing these metrics, you can get a better understanding of what type of content resonates with your audience and optimize your content strategy accordingly. TikTok also provides insights into trending content, which can help you stay on top of the latest trends and create content that resonates with your audience.

Tips for tracking your TikTok growth

Here are some tips for tracking your TikTok growth using the platform's built-in analytics:

Switch to a TikTok Pro Account: If you haven't already, consider switching to a TikTok Pro Account to access the platform's analytics. This will give you access to key metrics such as views, likes, comments, shares, follower count, and more.

Track Video Performance: Pay attention to the performance of your videos over time. Which videos are getting the most engagement and views? What types of content are resonating most with your audience? Use this information to guide your content strategy and create more of what's working.

Monitor Follower Growth: Keep an eye on your follower count and monitor growth over time. Look for patterns or spikes in follower growth to identify what content or strategies are driving new followers.

Analyze Audience Demographics: TikTok provides data on your audience demographics, including age, gender, and location. Use this information to better understand who your audience is and create content that resonates with them.

Pay Attention to Trends: TikTok is all about trends, so pay attention to what's trending and incorporate relevant trends into your content strategy. Use analytics to identify which trend-related content is performing best with your audience.

Experiment with Hashtags: Hashtags are a powerful way to boost your reach and increase visibility on TikTok. Experiment with different hashtags and track which ones are driving the most views and engagement.

Set Goals and Track Progress: Finally, set goals for your TikTok growth and regularly track your progress using analytics. Use this information to adjust your content strategy and tactics to continue growing your following and engagement.

How to use TikTok analytics to improve your content and strategy

To use TikTok analytics to improve your content and strategy, you should first track your key metrics over time to identify patterns and trends in your performance. Some key metrics to focus on include:

Views: The number of times your videos have been viewed.

Engagement: The number of likes, comments, shares, and follows your content has received.

Follower growth: The rate at which your followers are increasing over time.

Audience demographics: The age, gender, and location of your audience.

Once you have a clear understanding of your performance metrics, you can use this data to refine your content strategy. Here are some tips:

Analyze your top-performing videos: Look for common themes, such as types of content, hashtags, or captions that resonate with your audience. Use this information to create more content that follows these patterns.

Identify peak engagement times: Check the time of day and days of the week when your videos get the most engagement. Schedule your content to post during these times for maximum impact.

Experiment with new content formats: Try out new video formats, such as duets, challenges, or tutorials. See how your audience responds and adjust your strategy accordingly.

Monitor your follower growth: Keep an eye on your follower count and track how it changes in response to your content. This can help you identify what types of content your audience is most interested in.

Use trending hashtags and challenges: Keep an eye on popular hashtags and challenges and see how you can incorporate them into your content. This can help increase your visibility and reach new audiences.

By using TikTok analytics to monitor your performance and adjust your strategy accordingly, you can build a stronger presence on the platform and grow your following over time.

Chapter 7: Engaging with Your Audience

TikTok is not just a platform to post videos; it's a community that values engagement and connection. Therefore, it's crucial to engage with your audience and build relationships with them. In this chapter, we'll discuss tips and strategies for engaging with your TikTok audience.

Respond to comments: When people take the time to leave comments on your videos, make sure to respond to them. It's an excellent way to build a relationship with your followers and show that you value their feedback and support. Responding to comments also increases the visibility of your content, as it sends a signal to the TikTok algorithm that people are engaging with your videos.

Use the duet and stitch features: The duet and stitch features are great ways to collaborate with your followers and create engaging content. Duetting allows you to record a video alongside someone else's video, while stitching lets you add your own video to the end of someone else's video. By using these features, you can create fun and creative content that encourages your followers to engage with you and each other.

Host Q&A sessions: Hosting Q&A sessions is an effective way to interact with your audience and answer their questions. You can do this by either posting a video asking your followers to leave their questions in the comments or by using TikTok's "Questions" feature, which allows your followers to submit questions that you can answer in a video.

Participate in challenges: TikTok challenges are a fun way to engage with your audience and show off your creativity. By participating in challenges, you can encourage your followers to create and engage with your content while also increasing your visibility on the platform.

Use polls and surveys: Polls and surveys are great tools for engaging with your audience and collecting valuable feedback. You can use them to ask your followers about their preferences, opinions, and interests, and then use this information to create content that resonates with them.

Show behind-the-scenes content: Giving your audience a behind-the-scenes look at your life or your creative process is an excellent way to build a personal connection with them. By showing your followers the person behind the videos, you can make them feel more invested in your content and more likely to engage with you.

Engaging with your audience is a crucial part of building a successful brand on TikTok. By following these tips and strategies, you can create a loyal following of engaged and invested followers who are excited to see what you'll post next.

The importance of engaging with your TikTok audience

Engaging with your TikTok audience is crucial for building a strong following and establishing a loyal fan base. When you respond to comments and messages, you show your audience that you care about their thoughts and opinions, and you build a sense of community around your content.

Engagement can also help you improve your content and strategy. When you actively listen to feedback and pay attention to which videos perform well, you can adjust your approach and create more content that resonates with your audience.

Here are some tips for engaging with your TikTok audience:

Respond to comments: Take the time to respond to comments on your videos, even if it's just a quick "thank you!" or "glad you enjoyed the video." This shows your audience that you're paying attention and appreciate their support.

Ask for feedback: Encourage your audience to share their thoughts and opinions in the comments section. Ask them what they'd like to see more of, what they enjoy about your content, and what they think you could improve upon.

Host Q&A sessions: Consider hosting live Q&A sessions or responding to viewer questions in a dedicated video. This is a great way to build a stronger connection with your audience and give them a chance to get to know you better.

Collaborate with other creators: Collaborating with other creators can help you expand your reach and engage with new audiences. When you work with other creators, you can also tap into their fan base and build new connections.

Use polls and surveys: TikTok's built-in polling feature can be a fun way to engage your audience and get feedback on your content. Consider using polls and surveys to ask your audience what they'd like to see more of or get their thoughts on specific topics.

Remember, engagement is a two-way street. Make sure to take the time to show your audience that you value their support and opinions, and be open to feedback and suggestions. By building a strong relationship with your audience, you can create a community around your content and continue to grow your following on TikTok.

Tips for responding to comments and messages

Here are some tips for responding to comments and messages on TikTok:

Be timely: Respond to comments and messages as quickly as possible, ideally within 24 hours. This shows your audience that you value their engagement and feedback.

Be authentic: Respond in your own voice and show your personality. People follow creators on TikTok because they connect with their unique perspectives, so don't be afraid to be yourself.

Use emojis: Emojis are a great way to convey emotion and personality in a short message. Use them to add some fun and playfulness to your responses.

Ask questions: Encourage conversation by asking questions in response to comments. This can help deepen the relationship with your audience and foster a sense of community.

Avoid generic responses: Try to respond to each comment or message individually, rather than with a generic response. This can help your audience feel heard and appreciated.

Address negative comments with care: If you receive negative comments or criticism, respond with empathy and kindness. Don't engage in arguments or be defensive, as this can damage your reputation.

Take advantage of live streaming: Use TikTok's live streaming feature to connect with your audience in real time. This can be a great way to answer questions and engage with viewers directly.

Strategies for building a community on TikTok

Building a community on TikTok is a powerful way to grow your following and increase engagement on your content. Here are some tips for building a strong community on the platform:

Respond to comments: One of the best ways to build a community on TikTok is to respond to comments on your videos. This shows your audience that you appreciate their engagement and are actively listening to their feedback.

Use hashtags: Hashtags can help your content get discovered by people who are interested in your niche. Using relevant hashtags can help you reach a wider audience and connect with like-minded creators and viewers.

Participate in challenges: TikTok challenges are a great way to engage with other creators and build a sense of community around a specific topic or theme. Participating in challenges can help you connect with other creators, gain exposure, and build a following.

Host live streams: Hosting a live stream on TikTok can be a great way to interact with your audience in real time. You can answer questions, respond to comments, and provide exclusive content to your followers.

Collaborate with other creators: Collaborating with other creators can help you build relationships and reach a wider audience. By working together, you can create content that appeals to both of your audiences and build a stronger community.

Use the duet feature: The duet feature allows you to create a split-screen video with another TikTok user. This can be a great way to collaborate with other creators and engage with your audience in a new and creative way.

Show your personality: TikTok is a platform that values authenticity and personality. By showing your unique perspective and personality in your content, you can attract a loyal following and build a strong community around your brand.

Chapter 8: Promoting Your TikTok Account

Promotion is an essential part of growing your TikTok account. Here are some effective strategies to promote your TikTok account:

Share your TikTok videos on other social media platforms: Share your TikTok videos on other social media platforms like Instagram, Twitter, and Facebook. Make sure to use relevant hashtags and catchy captions to grab your audience's attention. You can also ask your followers to follow your TikTok account.

Collaborate with other TikTok creators: Collaborating with other TikTok creators is an excellent way to gain more exposure. When you collaborate with other creators, you can tap into their audience and gain more followers.

Participate in TikTok challenges: Participating in TikTok challenges is an excellent way to gain more exposure. When you participate in a challenge, your video will be visible to a wider audience, and you can gain more followers.

Engage with other TikTok users: Engaging with other TikTok users is an excellent way to build relationships and gain more followers. Leave comments on other users' videos, like and share their content, and respond to their comments on your videos.

Use relevant hashtags: Using relevant hashtags is an effective way to reach a wider audience. When you use relevant hashtags, your videos will be visible to people who are interested in the same topics.

Collaborate with brands: Collaborating with brands is an excellent way to gain more exposure and followers. When you collaborate with brands, you can tap into their audience and gain more followers.

Run a TikTok ad campaign: Running a TikTok ad campaign is an effective way to reach a wider audience. You can create an ad campaign to promote your TikTok account or a specific video.

Participate in TikTok events: TikTok hosts various events throughout the year, such as live streams and challenges. Participating in these events is an excellent way to gain more exposure and followers.

Cross-promote with other TikTok users: Cross-promoting with other TikTok users is an excellent way to gain more exposure. You can collaborate with other users to create a video and tag each other in the post.

In conclusion, promoting your TikTok account requires effort and creativity. By using the strategies mentioned above, you can gain more exposure, build relationships, and gain more followers.

Promoting your TikTok account on other social media platforms

One of the best ways to promote your TikTok account is by sharing your TikTok videos on other social media platforms. This way, you can reach a wider audience and potentially gain more followers.

Here are some tips for promoting your TikTok account on other social media platforms:

Share your TikTok videos on Instagram, Facebook, Twitter, and other social media platforms. You can also embed your TikTok videos on your website or blog.

Use relevant hashtags when you share your TikTok videos. This will help your videos reach people who are interested in the same topics as your content.

Collaborate with other social media influencers. Find other influencers in your niche who have a large following on other platforms and collaborate with them to promote each other's content.

Run a social media contest or giveaway. Encourage your followers on other platforms to follow you on TikTok by offering a prize or incentive.

Use paid social media advertising to promote your TikTok account. This can be a great way to quickly reach a large audience and gain new followers.

Utilizing TikTok ads to

increase your reach

Utilizing TikTok ads can be an effective way to increase your reach on the platform. TikTok offers several advertising options for businesses and creators, including:

In-Feed Ads: These are full-screen ads that appear in users' "For You" feeds. In-Feed ads can be up to 60 seconds long and can include a call-to-action button.

Brand Takeovers: These are full-screen ads that appear when a user opens the app. Brand Takeovers can include images, GIFs, or videos up to 15 seconds long.

Branded Hashtag Challenges: Brands can create their own hashtag challenges and promote them on the platform. TikTok users can participate in the challenge by creating their own videos using the hashtag.

Branded Effects: Brands can create their own custom filters, stickers, and augmented reality effects for users to incorporate into their videos.

When creating TikTok ads, it's important to consider your target audience and create content that resonates with them. Keep in mind that TikTok is a platform that values authenticity and creativity, so your ads should reflect this as well. It's also important to track the performance of your ads using TikTok's analytics tools to ensure that they are having the desired impact.

Tips for promoting your TikTok account offline

Promoting your TikTok account offline can be a great way to reach a wider audience and build your following. Here are some tips for promoting your TikTok account offline:

Use QR codes: Include a QR code on business cards, flyers, or other printed materials that people can scan to follow your TikTok account.

Host events: Host events or meetups where you can showcase your TikTok content and encourage people to follow your account.

Collaborate with local businesses: Partner with local businesses to promote your TikTok account. For example, you could offer to create TikTok videos for them in exchange for a shoutout on their social media channels.

Use merchandise: Create merchandise with your TikTok username on it, such as t-shirts or stickers, and wear/use them in public to promote your account.

Advertise in local media: Place ads in local newspapers, magazines, or other media outlets to promote your TikTok account.

Use guerrilla marketing: Get creative with your marketing efforts by using unconventional tactics such as chalk art or graffiti to promote your TikTok account in public spaces.

Speak at events: Offer to speak at events or conferences related to your niche or industry and use the opportunity to promote your

TikTok account.

Remember to always follow local laws and regulations when promoting your TikTok account offline.

Chapter 9: TikTok Etiquette and Community Guidelines

As with any social media platform, TikTok has its own set of community guidelines that users are expected to follow. These guidelines exist to ensure that the app remains a safe and welcoming space for everyone. In this chapter, we will discuss some of the most important community guidelines to be aware of, as well as some general TikTok etiquette tips.

Respect others' privacy: TikTok values the privacy of its users, and you should too. This means not sharing personal information, such as someone's phone number or address, without their explicit consent. Additionally, you should not record or post content of others without their consent.

Do not bully or harass others: TikTok has a zero-tolerance policy for bullying and harassment. This includes making derogatory comments about someone's race, gender, sexuality, or appearance, as well as threatening or intimidating behavior.

Avoid inappropriate content: TikTok is meant to be a family-friendly app, so it's important to keep your content appropriate for all ages. This means avoiding explicit language, sexual content, and graphic violence.

Respect intellectual property rights: It's important to respect the intellectual property rights of others. This means not posting content that you do not have the rights to, such as copyrighted music or videos.

Do not engage in spamming or phishing: TikTok does not tolerate spamming or phishing behavior. This means not using the app to send unsolicited messages or post spammy comments.

Follow community guidelines: Finally, it's important to read and follow TikTok's community guidelines. These guidelines are in place to ensure that the app remains a safe and positive space for everyone.

In addition to these community guidelines, there are also some general TikTok etiquette tips to keep in mind. For example:

Be respectful of other users: Just as you would in real life, it's important to be respectful of other TikTok users. This means not leaving derogatory comments, engaging in arguments, or otherwise being rude or disrespectful.

Engage with other users: TikTok is a social media platform, which means it's important to engage with other users. This means leaving comments on other users' videos, following them, and generally being an active and positive member of the TikTok community.

Stay true to yourself: Finally, it's important to stay true to yourself on TikTok. While it can be tempting to try to be someone, you're not in order to gain followers or likes, this is ultimately not sustainable. Instead, focus on creating content that is true to your personality and interests, and let your following grow naturally over time.

By following these TikTok etiquette tips and community guidelines, you can ensure that you are using the app in a responsible and positive way.

Understanding TikTok's community guidelines

TikTok's community guidelines outline the platform's rules and policies for content and behavior. These guidelines are designed to ensure that TikTok remains a safe and positive environment for all users. Violating these guidelines can result in content removal, account suspension, and even legal action in some cases.

TikTok's community guidelines cover a range of topics, including:

Harmful content: TikTok prohibits content that promotes violence, hate speech, harassment, bullying, or harmful activities such as self-harm, drug abuse, or animal cruelty.

Misinformation: TikTok prohibits the spread of false information, such as conspiracy theories or hoaxes.

Nudity and sexual content: TikTok prohibits explicit or sexually suggestive content.

Dangerous activities: TikTok prohibits content that depicts dangerous or risky behavior, such as stunts or challenges that could cause harm.

Intellectual property: TikTok prohibits the use of copyrighted material without permission, including music, images, and videos.

Privacy: TikTok requires users to respect the privacy of others and prohibits the sharing of personal information without consent.

Community norms: TikTok expects users to follow community norms, such as not engaging in spamming or creating fake accounts.

It is important to read and understand TikTok's community guidelines before creating content on the platform. Users should also be aware that the guidelines are subject to change, and it is their responsibility to stay up-to-date with any updates or changes.

Best practices for following TikTok etiquette

Here are some best practices for following TikTok etiquette:

Respect other users: TikTok is a community of people from all over the world with different backgrounds and beliefs. It is important to treat others with respect and avoid any hate speech, bullying, or harassment.

Follow the community guidelines: TikTok has strict guidelines about what is allowed on the platform. Familiarize yourself with these guidelines and make sure your content follows them.

Give credit where credit is due: If you use someone else's content, give them credit in your video or caption. This shows respect for the original creator and can also help you connect with others in the community.

Avoid spamming: Avoid spamming other users with comments, messages, or content. This can come across as pushy or annoying and may result in others blocking or reporting your account.

Engage with the community: Engage with other users by commenting on their videos, responding to comments on your own videos, and participating in challenges and trends. This can help you build relationships and grow your following.

Be authentic: TikTok is all about authenticity, so be yourself and share content that is true to who you are. Avoid trying to be someone you're not or creating content that goes against your values or beliefs.

By following these best practices, you can help create a positive and supportive community on TikTok while also growing your following and achieving your goals on the platform.

Avoiding common mistakes and pitfalls on TikTok

Here are some common mistakes and pitfalls to avoid on TikTok:

Violating community guidelines: Make sure to review TikTok's community guidelines and follow them strictly to avoid being banned or restricted on the platform.

Not engaging with your audience: TikTok is a social media platform, and engagement is crucial. Take the time to respond to comments and messages to build a relationship with your followers.

Focusing only on views and likes: While views and likes are important metrics, they aren't the only ones that matter. Make sure to track other metrics like shares, comments, and watch time to get a more complete picture of your performance.

Ignoring trends and challenges: Trends and challenges are a big part of TikTok culture. While it's important to find your own niche, make sure to keep an eye on what's trending and consider participating in popular challenges.

Posting too infrequently or too often: Finding the right posting frequency can be a challenge, but it's important to find a balance that works for you and your audience. Posting too infrequently can make it hard to gain traction, while posting too often can lead to oversaturation and a drop in engagement.

Being too promotional: While promoting your products or services on TikTok is okay, it's important not to be too promotional. Instead, focus on creating engaging content that provides value to your followers.

Using inappropriate language or imagery: TikTok is a family-friendly platform, and using inappropriate language or imagery can result in a ban or restriction. Make sure to keep your content clean and appropriate for all ages.

Not optimizing your content for the algorithm: The TikTok algorithm is a key part of the platform, and optimizing your content for it can help increase your visibility and reach. Make sure to use relevant hashtags, participate in challenges, and post at optimal times for your audience.

By avoiding these mistakes and pitfalls, you can increase your chances of success on TikTok and build a strong following on the platform.

Chapter 10: Conclusion

In conclusion, TikTok has quickly become one of the most popular social media platforms in the world, with over a billion active users. For businesses and creators, TikTok presents a unique opportunity to build a following and engage with a diverse audience.

To succeed on TikTok, it's important to understand how the algorithm works, what type of content performs well, and how to create a consistent brand image. Collaborating with other TikTok creators and engaging with your audience are also key strategies for building your following.

By leveraging TikTok analytics, promoting your account on other platforms, and following TikTok's community guidelines, you can maximize your chances of success on the platform.

Remember that TikTok is constantly evolving, so it's important to stay up to date with the latest trends and best practices to ensure your continued growth and success. With dedication and effort, TikTok can be a powerful tool for building your brand and reaching a global audience.

The potential for growth and success on TikTok

TikTok is an incredibly powerful platform for building a following, promoting your brand, and creating engaging content. With its rapidly growing user base and easy-to-use tools, it offers unparalleled potential for growth and success.

By understanding the TikTok algorithm, creating engaging content, building a strong brand, collaborating with other creators, and utilizing analytics and engagement strategies, you can build a devoted following and achieve your goals on the platform.

However, it's important to remember that success on TikTok takes time, effort, and dedication. By following the tips and best practices outlined in this guide, you can maximize your potential and make the most of your TikTok experience.

So don't be afraid to experiment, try new things, and engage with your audience. With the right strategy and approach, TikTok can be a powerful tool for achieving your goals and building your brand.

Final tips and advice for building your TikTok following

Here are some final tips and advice for building your TikTok following:

Stay Consistent: Consistency is key when it comes to growing your TikTok account. Make sure you post regularly and keep your content fresh and engaging.

Experiment with Different Types of Content: Don't be afraid to experiment with different types of content to see what resonates with your audience. Try out different trends and challenges and see what works best for you.

Engage with Your Audience: Engage with your audience by responding to comments, messages, and duet requests. Building a community on TikTok is all about engagement.

Collaborate with Other Creators: Collaborating with other TikTok creators can help you reach new audiences and grow your following.

Utilize TikTok Analytics: Make use of TikTok's analytics to track your growth and improve your content and strategy.

Promote Your TikTok Account: Promote your TikTok account on other social media platforms and offline to increase your reach.

Follow TikTok's Community Guidelines: Make sure you follow TikTok's community guidelines and etiquette to avoid any issues or penalties.

By following these tips and consistently putting in effort, you can build a strong and engaged following on TikTok. Remember, it takes time and effort, but with patience and persistence, you can achieve great success on this platform.

The future of TikTok and its role in the social media landscape

TikTok has rapidly grown to become one of the most popular social media platforms worldwide, with millions of users creating and sharing content on the platform every day. As the platform continues to evolve and innovate, it is likely that it will play an even bigger role in the social media landscape in the coming years.

One trend that is likely to continue is the increased use of video content. As more and more users flock to TikTok, other social media platforms are also looking to incorporate more video content into their offerings. This means that TikTok's influence is likely to continue to grow and shape the direction of the social media industry as a whole.

Another trend that is likely to continue is the increasing importance of influencers and creators on the platform. As brands and businesses continue to look for ways to reach younger audiences, they will increasingly turn to influencers and creators who have built a following on TikTok. This means that creators will continue to have significant power and influence on the platform, and will likely be able to monetize their content more effectively in the future.

Finally, as the platform continues to grow and evolve, it is likely that we will see more sophisticated tools and features for creators and businesses. TikTok is already testing e-commerce integrations and other features that could make it easier for brands to sell products directly to consumers on the platform. As these tools become more widespread, TikTok will likely become an even more attractive platform for businesses and creators alike.

Overall, the future of TikTok looks bright. With its massive user base, innovative features, and growing influence, the platform is poised to become an even more important part of the social media landscape in the coming years. By following the tips and strategies outlined in this book, you can position yourself for success and growth on TikTok.

T ikTok offers a unique opportunity for businesses and creators to reach a vast and diverse audience. By understanding the algorithm, creating engaging content, building a strong brand, collaborating with other creators, utilizing analytics, engaging with your audience, and promoting your account, you can successfully build your following on TikTok.

As with any social media platform, it's essential to follow the community guidelines and etiquette, avoid common mistakes and pitfalls, and stay up to date with the latest trends and changes.

The future of TikTok looks bright, with the platform's continued growth and potential for innovation. By leveraging the power of TikTok, you can achieve significant growth and success for yourself or your business.

www.ingramcontent.com/pod-product-compliance
Lightning Source LLC
Chambersburg PA
CBHW070459220526

45466CB00004B/1887